Fork in the Chalkboard: Futures of American Public Education

Written by
Derek Setser

To my students; past, present, and future.
Your curiosity, courage, and questions are the heartbeat of this work.

To my wife (Kaci), son (José), and daughter (Addison).
Thank you for your love, patience, and unwavering belief in the value of this journey.

And to every young scholar whose path to education was blocked, narrowed, or denied.
May this book stand as both witness and invitation. You deserve to learn, to dream, to lead.

Table of Contents

Title	Page Number
Author's Note	1
Introduction	3
Chapter 1 The Privatized Nation	5
Chapter 2 Microschool America	16
Chapter 3 AI Replaces Us	26
Chapter 4 The Resilient Commons	36
Chapter 5 Surveillance Schools	46
Chapter 6 Educator Exodus	56
Chapter 7 Democratic Renaissance	66
Chapter 8 The Fight We Choose	76
A Blueprint in Fragments	86
What You Can Do Next?	87
Blueprints for Action	88
Resource List: Tools for the Fight Ahead	109
Call to Collective Action	112
My Commitments to Public Education	113

Table of Contents cont.

Title	Page Number
Facilitation Guide for Book Clubs & Communities	114
Glossary	117
References	118

Author's Note: Why I Wrote This Book

"This book is not a neutral project.

It was written because public education in the United States is at a crossroads, one where silence is complicity, and clarity is urgently needed. I wrote it because every day, educators, students, families, and local leaders are being pulled into a manufactured crisis designed to erode trust in public schools and shift control into private hands. Too often, the people living these stories are kept from shaping the narrative.

I wrote this book because I am one of those people. As an educator, I have witnessed the harm caused by disinvestment, misinformation, burnout, and policy decisions that treat schools as test sites rather than communities. As a professional working inside this system, I have seen the gap between what is said and what is done, between the public promises and the lived realities. But more importantly, I have seen what is possible when people organize.

This book is not meant to offer easy answers. It is not an academic exposition. It is a tool, a provocation, a mirror. It presents eight future scenarios, each grounded in current policy trends, political shifts, and economic interests. Some will feel alarmingly close. Others may seem unlikely; until they are not.

The goal is not prediction. The goal is preparation. If public education is to remain truly public, then it must be defended, reimagined, and rebuilt by the very people it serves. That includes students, families, educators, advocates, board members, organizers, and you.

You may not agree with everything in this book. That is expected. What I hope is that you leave these pages asking sharper questions, noticing deeper patterns, and committing to action that aligns with your values.

This is not a call to nostalgia. It is a call to participation.

Because the future of public education is not written yet. But it will be.

And we are the ones who will write it." - Derek Setser

Introduction: Which Future Will We Choose?

A school shuts down in rural North Carolina. A microschool opens in an urban garage. A chatbot teaches third graders in a city classroom. A school board meeting erupts into shouting over banned books. All in the same week. These are not isolated events, they are signals of something deeper, more volatile, and far more urgent.

Public education in America is not simply in crisis. It is being redefined, actively, aggressively, and unevenly, by forces that span political ideologies, corporate interests, grassroots movements, and everyday exhaustion. The questions are no longer about whether the system is working. The questions are: "For whom is it working?" "Who is shaping its future?" And "who will be left behind when it arrives?"

This book is not a forecast. It is a map of possibilities. It offers a series of scenarios, eight distinct futures of public education, that reflect the decisions we are making right now, knowingly or not. Some are dystopian. Some are visionary. All are grounded in real data, current events, and lived experiences from classrooms, boardrooms, and kitchen tables across the country.

Each chapter pairs a fictionalized vignette with factual analysis and real-world policy trajectories. These are not predictions. They are warnings and invitations. You will meet students learning under corporate loyalty banners, families running microschools from their garages, AI programs replacing certified teachers, and communities rising from the ashes of disinvestment to rebuild schools as democratic commons. None of these futures are fantasy. All of them are plausible. Some are already here.

Public education is more than a set of policies or performance metrics. It is a public trust, a fragile, foundational institution where democracy is supposed to be lived, not just taught. It is where we decide whether children will grow up to memorize facts or to question power; to recite pledges or to reimagine systems.

In this moment of competing narratives and colliding realities, we face a choice. We can surrender public education to privatization, automation, and control. Or we can reclaim it, rebuild it as a site of justice, care, and collective power.

This book does not end with a single answer. It ends with the truth that the future is not something we inherit, it is something we choose, together.

Let us see what paths we have made, and which ones we are ready to walk.

Welcome to the crossroads.

Disclaimer on Vignettes

The people you meet in these pages (Amira, Elijah, Kyla, Ms. Thompson, Zara, Jamal, and others) are not portraits of actual individuals. They are composite characters, drawn from patterns, research, and countless stories shared by educators, families, and students across the country. Their names, schools, and circumstances are fictionalized to protect privacy, while their struggles and hopes echo the very real experiences shaping public education today.

These vignettes are mirrors and metaphors, designed to bring policy trends into human focus. Any resemblance to actual persons, schools, or districts is purely coincidental. The truths here are systemic, not personal.

CHAPTER 1: THE PRIVATIZED NATION

"PUBLIC DOLLARS, PRIVATE DREAMS"

Scenario Overview:

This scenario explores what happens when public education is transformed into a marketplace. Rooted in 20th-century school choice rhetoric and accelerated by 21st-century voucher expansion, the idea of privatizing education began with Milton Friedman's proposals in the 1950s. It was later championed by political groups advocating for deregulation, religious schooling, and the dismantling of teachers' unions. Today, key drivers include conservative think tanks like the Heritage Foundation, pro-voucher legislators in state governments, and billionaire-funded advocacy groups such as American Federation for Children. These entities push for Education Savings Accounts (ESAs) and universal voucher systems, often under the language of "parental rights" and "educational freedom."

The beneficiaries of this model are private school networks, corporate education providers, and ideological groups seeking control over curriculum. Meanwhile, families without financial means or logistical flexibility, especially students with disabilities, multilingual learners, and those in rural or urban under-resourced districts, face exclusion, instability, and discrimination.

Unchecked, this trend fragments education into competitive, commodified silos. The result is a landscape where equity is abandoned, public oversight evaporates, and students are treated as future employees rather than informed citizens. This chapter imagines that future fully realized.

"We do not call them schools anymore. We call them hubs. Each one has a sponsor, a slogan, and a loyalty app."

Narrative Vignette

Amira wakes to the soft buzz of her charter-issued smartband. It is Tuesday, which means she reports to the STEM Hub, two bus rides away from her apartment. Her older brother, Isaiah, goes in the opposite direction, to the Moral Leadership Academy. Their mom jokes that they are getting brand loyalty before breakfast. The joke is not funny anymore.

Their neighborhood school closed five years ago, phased out when the state enacted universal voucher legislation. It was labeled a "failure" after years of underfunding and student flight. Now, families like Amira's scramble each semester to reapply for limited seats in whichever corporate-sponsored institutions still accept state vouchers.

At the Hub, Amira swipes in, is facially scanned, and gets routed to a workstation. There are no teachers, just AI facilitators and a rotating team of para-educators. Her individualized algorithm determines the day's modules, quizzes, and feedback. Her progress is compared not only to district standards but also to STEM Hub's quarterly benchmarks for productivity. The screen flashes a reminder: "Learn Fast, Think Smart, Your Future is Our Fuel."

Unpacking the Scenario

This future is rooted in current efforts to dismantle public education under the banner of "parental choice" and "educational freedom." By 2025, over a dozen U.S. states had adopted universal voucher programs, funneling public money into private, often religious or for-profit schools with minimal oversight. In North Carolina, similar policies passed amid claims they would empower families, yet the data told a different story.

When vouchers expanded, the most vulnerable students, those with disabilities, language needs, or economic instability, were left behind in public schools stripped of funding. As enrollment dropped, neighborhood schools were closed or converted into charters. Corporations filled the vacuum, offering branded education in exchange for taxpayer dollars and a captive future workforce.

This scenario is a logical extension of that trend: the death of the public school as a shared civic institution, replaced by privatized hubs that serve as talent pipelines for their sponsors.

Data Snapshot

- In 2024, Arizona's ESA program exceeded $600 million in taxpayer spending, despite limited academic or financial accountability (Office of the Arizona Governor, 2024).
- In 2023, more than 40% of new voucher recipients in Florida were already attending private schools before receiving public funds, raising concerns about equity and resource diversion (Florida Policy Institute, 2023).
- A 2023 report found that voucher-funded schools routinely denied services or admission to students with disabilities, often citing exemption from federal requirements (Southern Poverty Law Center & Education Law Center, 2023).
- North Carolina experienced over 3,500 teacher vacancies in the 2023-2024 school year, with contributing factors including stagnant salaries and the redirection of public funds to private schools (EdNC, 2024).

Voices from the Field

"They said choice would lift all boats. But they sank ours to build yachts for everyone else." - Marcus L., former social studies teacher, Winston-Salem, NC

"My school has uniforms, tablets, and ads during morning announcements. But I have not had a counselor in three years." - Jazmin R., 10th grade student, Atlanta, GA

"Parents thought they would get control. What they got was a confusing, competitive marketplace where loyalty points mean more than learning." - Laila R., parent advocate, Houston, TX

Consequences

Equity Breakdown: Wealthier families game the system; marginalized families are left with the scraps.

While marketed as a tool for empowerment, voucher systems often tilt in favor of those who already have access. Wealthier families, with the time, transportation, and knowledge to navigate complex application processes, are well-positioned to capitalize on public subsidies. Meanwhile, marginalized families, particularly those facing economic hardship, language barriers, or systemic discrimination, are left navigating fewer options with greater obstacles. What is framed as "choice" often ends up reinforcing the very inequities it claims to solve.

Accountability Void: No consistent curriculum, standards, or protections for students.

Beneath the promise of innovation lies a patchwork system with no consistent curriculum, no shared academic standards, and no universal protections for students. Private schools receiving public funds are often not required to follow state assessments, report outcomes transparently, or adhere to civil rights protections applied in public education. For families, this creates a high-stakes guessing game; for students, it means vastly different experiences depending on which door they walk through, without any guarantee of support, oversight, or recourse when things go wrong. One North Carolina parent shared that her son, who has ADHD, was expelled from a private voucher school after just six weeks. No documentation. No hearing. No path for appeal. Public dollars funded the experience, public accountability was nowhere to be found.

Civic Collapse: Without shared public education, communities become ideologically and economically siloed.

When public education fragments, so does the civic fabric that binds communities together. Without shared schools, families retreat into ideological and economic silos, neighborhoods once united by common bell schedules, school plays, and PTA meetings give way to privatized bubbles and competing realities. Dialogue becomes harder. Trust erodes. Children grow up with fewer opportunities to learn alongside peers who look, live, or believe differently. In the absence of shared public institutions, the idea of a shared public future becomes harder to imagine, and even harder to fight for.

In one small Southern town, two schools sit just three miles apart: one is a legacy public school struggling with underfunding, the other a new private academy thriving on state vouchers. They serve the same zip code, but the children do not know each other's names. Their parents do not vote on the same issues. When a local library faced closure, turnout was low, because fewer people felt like it still belonged to them.

Workforce Capture: Education becomes narrowly tailored to employer needs, not student growth.

As public education becomes increasingly shaped by corporate interests, the purpose of schooling shifts, from nurturing well-rounded citizens to producing efficient, compliant workers. Curricula narrow. Critical thinking and civic engagement give way to job-readiness modules, personality assessments, and branded career pathways. Students are sorted not by potential but by perceived economic value. One district piloted a program where middle schoolers were funneled into industry-sponsored tracks based on algorithmic surveys, without input from families or educators. It is sold as opportunity. But when education is engineered to serve labor markets instead of learners, we lose not just imagination, we lose democracy.

Teacher Displacement: Certified teachers are replaced by cheaper labor and automation.

As budgets tighten and technology advances, a growing number of schools are opting to replace certified educators with less expensive labor or algorithmic alternatives. In some districts, paraprofessionals and contract-based "facilitators" now oversee online learning labs where AI tutors do most of the teaching. Certification requirements are relaxed, teaching assistants are asked to manage full classrooms, and corporations offer "turnkey" instructional platforms that claim to reduce the need for trained staff altogether. One charter network in the Southwest now employs more software engineers than credentialed teachers. The message is clear: efficiency over expertise. But when educators are pushed out, what disappears is not just instruction, it is mentorship, trust, cultural knowledge, and care.

What Could Be Done

- Reinvest in public schools as centers of community life.
- Pass federal regulations to ensure voucher-funded schools meet civil rights and academic standards.
- Create accountability systems that value student wellbeing, not just corporate outcomes.
- Mobilize teachers, parents, and students to demand transparency and reinstate public trust.

The future of education is a choice, not just for parents, but for society. Do we want a system where companies educate children for their own ends? Or a system that prepares children to lead, question, and change the world?

CHAPTER 2:

MICROSCHOOL AMERICA

Scenario Overview:

This scenario explores a decentralized future in which families create and run their own micro-learning environments outside traditional public systems. The microschool concept has roots in the homeschooling movement of the 1970s, gaining steam with unschooling and Montessori-inspired philosophies. But its current resurgence began during the COVID-19 pandemic, when school closures and dissatisfaction with remote learning pushed families, particularly those with resources, to experiment with alternative models.

Today, microschools are often funded and encouraged by organizations like the VELA Education Fund, with backing from philanthropists and tech-sector disruptors who promote "education innovation." Legislation in states like Arizona, Florida, and North Carolina has expanded access to Education Savings Accounts (ESAs), allowing public funds to be used for private, loosely regulated education pods. While marketed as "flexible" and "personalized," the microschool movement is rapidly becoming a tool for privatization.

Winners include affluent families who can afford to build or join well-resourced microschools, private curriculum vendors, and libertarian education reform groups. At risk are low-income families who lack time, credentials, or space to create alternatives, leading to further educational stratification.

If left unchecked, this model could result in a fractured education landscape: hyper-local, unevenly regulated, and deeply unequal. The promise of innovation risks becoming a mask for abandonment. This chapter imagines that possibility brought to scale.

"We did not leave public education. It left us."

Narrative Vignette

Elijah's classroom is a barn. Literally. Every morning, he helps feed goats and turn compost before joining seven other students around a kitchen table. Their teacher, Ms. Mae, is a retired biologist turned community educator. Today's lesson? Measuring water quality in a nearby creek and designing a system to filter it with natural materials. Elijah records his findings in a field journal.

There are no standardized tests here. No cafeteria trays. No state benchmarks. Parents fund the collective through monthly dues and manage logistics through a shared Google Doc. On Thursdays, the group meets with two other microschools for a community potluck and science fair.

Microschooling was not Plan A. Elijah's mom pulled him from public school after years of overcrowded classrooms, staff turnover, and curriculum restrictions. She wanted something real. Something grounded. Something human. What started as desperation became reinvention.

Unpacking the Scenario

Microschools are small, often parent-led or privately operated learning environments that serve a handful of students outside the traditional public or charter system. They are flexible, interest-driven, and usually untethered from state mandates.

In recent years, the exodus from public education has accelerated. Teacher shortages, culture wars, and political censorship pushed families to seek alternatives. COVID-19 normalized remote and hybrid learning, laying the groundwork for microschools to scale.

By the early 2020s, microschools exploded across the country, especially in states where deregulation opened the floodgates. Education became hyper-local and fragmented. Innovation thrived. Equity did not.

Data Snapshot

- As of 2024, an estimated 2.2 to 3.1 million students in the United States were homeschooled, depending on the source, reflecting sustained growth post-pandemic (National Home Education Research Institute, 2023; NCES, 2023).
- The VELA Education Fund, a leading microschool grantmaker, reported funding over 2,000 microlearning environments by the end of 2023, supporting educational entrepreneurs across the country (VELA Education Fund, 2023).
- In North Carolina, expanded Education Savings Accounts and Opportunity Scholarships allowed families to redirect public education funds to private and non-traditional schooling options, despite concerns about oversight and equity (AP News, 2023).
- Surveys and studies show that Black, Indigenous, and rural families are among the fastest-growing demographics within the homeschooling and microschooling movements; often driven by safety concerns, racial equity, and dissatisfaction with public schooling, rather than ideology (Ray, 2023; Time, 2022; Hamilton, 2023).

Voices from the Field

"I did not want to teach my kids. I had to." - Shannon W., single mother, Detroit, MI

"Microschools gave my students freedom. But they also gave me anxiety. There is no safety net if something goes wrong." - Luis M., community educator, Austin, TX

"The idea of 'school' as one-size-fits-all? That is over. But now we are all inventing the wheel from scratch." - Dr. Priya N., education researcher, Eugene, OR

Consequences

Innovation without Guardrails: Creativity blossoms, but there is no guarantee of quality, safety, or inclusivity.

In the absence of regulation and oversight, a surge of microschools, learning pods, and family-led co-ops has led to bursts of creativity and customization, but without any assurance of quality, safety, or inclusivity. Some families design rich, interdisciplinary learning environments; others rely on unvetted online programs or ideologically driven materials. While this freedom can feel empowering, it also means there is no baseline for what students should learn, how they are protected, or whether their rights are upheld. One parent's innovation may be another child's isolation. In a fragmented system, brilliance and neglect often sit side by side, and no one is obligated to notice the difference.

Parental Burnout: The burden of planning, teaching, and funding shifts entirely to families.

In microschool and homeschool ecosystems, the promise of autonomy often comes with a hidden cost, exhaustion. Without the support structures of traditional schools, parents must take on the roles of teacher, curriculum designer, administrator, and funder. For many, especially single parents or working-class families, this shift becomes unsustainable. Planning lessons at night, facilitating instruction by day, and navigating academic standards without guidance leaves families overwhelmed and isolated. What begins as empowerment can quickly devolve into stress, guilt, and fatigue. And when families burn out, there is often no safety net waiting to catch the students caught in the middle.

Equity Erosion: Wealthier communities create robust collectives. Poorer communities struggle to access materials, credentials, or time.

As microschools and co-ops flourish in pockets of the country, a stark divide emerges. Wealthier communities form robust educational collectives, hiring certified teachers, curating advanced curricula, and offering enrichment opportunities that rival private schools. Meanwhile, lower-income families often lack access to high-quality materials, internet connectivity, safe learning environments, or even the time to facilitate instruction. Without public infrastructure or equitable funding, the microschool movement risks becoming another engine of stratification. Education becomes not a right, but a luxury shaped by zip code, network, and disposable income.

Loss of Civic Common Ground: Children grow up in isolated learning pods, disconnected from broader society.

As children grow up in isolated learning pods, private microschools, and home-based co-ops, the shared experiences that once anchored communities begin to unravel. There are no school assemblies, no cross-cultural lunch tables, no common books or debates that stretch across classrooms. Students may thrive academically in niche environments, but at the cost of exposure to differing perspectives, collective challenges, and the messy, vital work of democratic coexistence. Over time, these educational silos do not just fragment learning, they fracture empathy. When students are taught apart, they grow apart, and the capacity to build a common future erodes with each disconnected year.

Policy Vacuum: States fail to regulate microschools effectively, leading to educational wild west.

As microschools proliferate, they often operate in a regulatory gray area, leading to a fragmented educational landscape. In many states, these institutions are not required to adhere to standardized curricula, teacher certification, or student assessment protocols. For instance, in Texas, microschools function with significant autonomy under homeschooling laws, facing minimal state oversight. Conversely, in New York, outdated homeschooling regulations can criminalize collaborative educational efforts among families, stifling innovation. This patchwork of policies results in inconsistent educational quality and accountability, leaving families navigating an "educational wild west" without clear guidelines or protections.

What Could Be Done

- Create hybrid public-micro partnerships that give families flexibility while preserving equity.
- Fund community-based learning hubs with certified educators and wraparound services.
- Establish minimum standards for microschool operations, safety, and curriculum.
- Reimagine public schools to offer personalized, localized learning within a shared civic framework.

Microschools reflect both a creative renaissance and a systemic failure. They are what happens when communities take education into their own hands, because no one else will. The question is not whether they will exist, but whether they will deepen division or inspire transformation.

CHAPTER 3:

AI REPLACES US

"WHEN ALGORITHMS TEACH THE CHILDREN"

Scenario Overview:

This scenario imagines a future where artificial intelligence replaces much of the instructional and emotional labor traditionally done by teachers. The origins of this vision stretch back to early educational technology in the 1980s and 1990s, but its rapid acceleration began with machine learning breakthroughs in the 2010s and was fast-tracked by the remote learning crisis during the COVID-19 pandemic. Companies like Khan Academy, Pearson, and edtech startups, often backed by venture capital, began integrating AI into instruction, assessment, and behavior management.

The current push comes from edtech giants, budget-strapped districts, and state legislatures seeking to "modernize" schooling while reducing labor costs. Framed as personalized, data-driven, and efficient, these systems often mask their primary function: cost-cutting through automation.

The primary beneficiaries are technology companies, AI developers, and policymakers under pressure to cut public expenditures. Those most at risk are students in underfunded schools, neurodivergent learners, and communities already experiencing teacher shortages, who are more likely to be assigned AI instructors instead of human educators.

Unchecked, this trend leads to the dehumanization of learning. Students are reduced to data points, teachers become obsolete, and education becomes transactional rather than relational. This chapter explores what it means to be educated by machines in a world that has chosen efficiency over empathy.

"Efficiency is not empathy."

Narrative Vignette

Kyla stares at the screen. Her adaptive tutor, a sleek, voice-optimized AI named Aristo, has just given her a 4.2 out of 5 on her reading comprehension. She tries to click for feedback, but it only offers a generic message: "Improve focus. Revisit inference module." Her real question, why the story made her feel sad, goes unanswered.

Her classroom has no teacher. Not really. A learning facilitator oversees thirty students moving through individualized AI-curated playlists. Behavioral data is collected in real time. Kyla's blinking rate is flagged. Her fidgeting triggers a soft prompt: "Are you focused? Take a break if needed."

Her dad, a former English teacher, now manages a local warehouse. He left the classroom two years ago when the district replaced 60% of its staff with learning automation systems. He calls the new model "cold learning." Kyla doesn't know what it's like to raise her hand and ask a human for help.

Unpacking the Scenario

This future emerges from a collision of two accelerating forces: the teacher shortage crisis and the rapid development of artificial intelligence in education. By 2025, schools across the U.S. were experimenting with AI tutors, grading bots, and predictive analytics platforms. Some were pitched as tools to support teachers. Others quietly replaced them.

Districts facing budget shortfalls began outsourcing instruction to edtech platforms that promised personalization, cost-savings, and round-the-clock availability. But what got lost in the algorithm was the heart of teaching, relationships, mentorship, nuance, and the ability to respond to student emotion or confusion in real time.

AI can process data. It cannot care.

Data Snapshot

- As of 2024, approximately 48% of U.S. school districts had trained educators on the use of AI tools for grading, instruction, or behavioral monitoring, marking a significant rise from the previous year (Doan et al., 2024).
- The global market for AI in education is expected to grow from $5.88 billion in 2024 to over $32 billion by 2030, driven by demand for personalized learning platforms and predictive analytics (Grand View Research, 2024).
- In North Carolina, state education officials released new guidance in 2024 on implementing generative AI in classrooms, encouraging pilot programs for AI-assisted instruction across multiple grade levels (North Carolina Department of Public Instruction [NCDPI], 2024).
- A 2023 RAND Corporation study reported that students in AI-facilitated classrooms performed comparably to peers on assessments but experienced lower engagement and elevated stress levels, particularly in fully automated environments (Doan et al., 2023).

Voices from the Field

"It's not teaching. It's managing tabs." - Chris H., classroom facilitator, Atlanta, GA

"My daughter talks to her chatbot more than any adult at school." - Dana R., parent, Charlotte, NC

"The tech is impressive. But without humans, it's just noise, fast, efficient, unfeeling noise." - Raul G., former principal, Austin, TX

Consequences

Dehumanization: Students feel unseen, unheard, and emotionally detached from learning.

In classrooms dominated by AI tutors and algorithm-driven pacing tools, students report feeling unseen and unheard. Lessons adjust to speed and accuracy, not emotion or curiosity. Eye contact is replaced by engagement metrics. Struggles are flagged but rarely understood. The warmth of a teacher's encouragement, the subtle affirmation of being known, these disappear behind dashboards and avatars. One 7th grader described their school day as "just checking boxes until the screen turns green." The result is not just academic detachment, it is emotional withdrawal from the entire concept of learning.

Depersonalized Discipline: Behavior tracking and predictive analytics replace restorative practices.

Predictive analytics and behavior-tracking platforms now claim to identify "at-risk" students before conflict even occurs. Facial expression scanners, tone analyzers, and keystroke monitors feed into disciplinary algorithms that flag potential noncompliance. In some schools, students receive demerits for being "off-task" without human interaction or conversation. Restorative practices, once a bridge to understanding, are replaced by automated alerts and parent emails. Students are left to navigate digital judgment without dialogue, reflection, or repair. Accountability becomes one-sided, and relationships become optional.

Teacher Exodus: Automation accelerates staff reductions, deskilling the profession.

As AI platforms replace direct instruction, districts see an opportunity to cut costs by reducing certified staff. Some roles shift to tech facilitators or part-time monitors; others disappear entirely. The profession is hollowed out, less about pedagogy, more about troubleshooting software and supervising screens. For many teachers, the shift feels like being slowly erased. Experienced educators leave, citing a loss of autonomy and purpose. The craft of teaching, mentorship, improvisation, deep content knowledge, gets treated as a luxury, not a necessity. What remains is a skeleton crew overseeing scripted systems.

Data Dependency: Learning becomes optimized for what can be measured, compliance, speed, and correctness, at the expense of creativity and inquiry.

In AI-powered classrooms, learning is defined by what can be captured and quantified. Platforms reward compliance, speed, and correctness, often at the expense of deeper inquiry, reflection, or creativity. Writing that explores nuance may score lower than a rigidly structured response. A student who asks "why" too often may be flagged for being off-task. Over time, the feedback loop narrows both instruction and imagination. Students learn to perform for metrics rather than to wonder, wrestle, or construct meaning. And when growth becomes a number on a dashboard, the soul of learning risks vanishing entirely.

Equity Risks: Affluent families opt out or supplement with live educators; marginalized students are left with machines.

As automated learning models spread, so does the digital divide. Affluent families can afford to opt out, enrolling in private schools with live educators, or layering AI tools with personal tutors and enrichment programs. Meanwhile, underfunded schools often implement these systems as a cost-saving measure, offering the illusion of innovation without meaningful human interaction. For marginalized students, this creates a new form of segregation: one where some learn through relationships, and others learn alone. The result is not equal opportunity, it's a quiet entrenchment of inequity disguised as tech advancement.

What Could Be Done

- Establish guardrails: Limit automation to support roles, not instructional replacement.
- Enforce transparency and consent for AI-based student data collection.
- Reinvest in teacher training focused on tech integration that enhances, not replaces, human teaching.
- Promote learning models that prioritize human connection, creativity, and community.

Technology is a tool, not a teacher. The future of education cannot be reduced to algorithms and analytics. To raise whole humans, we need whole educators.

CHAPTER 4:
THE RESILIENT COMMONS

"RECLAIMING EDUCATION AS A PUBLIC ACT"

Scenario Overview:

This scenario envisions a future where communities take back control of education by reclaiming public school buildings, repurposing them into hubs of learning, wellness, and civic life. The concept of schools as "community anchors" dates back to the settlement house movement of the early 20th century and re-emerged during the 1960s civil rights era. However, in the face of modern privatization, school closures, and strict policies, this vision has resurfaced as a grassroots counter-movement to the dismantling of public institutions.

The push behind this scenario comes not from centralized policy, but from the ground up, educators, students, mutual aid networks, neighborhood coalitions, and public sector unions who refuse to let schools become hollow shells or privatized commodities. In some cases, progressive city councils, foundations, and universities have supported this reclamation. But mostly, it is communities doing what policymakers would not.

Beneficiaries include entire neighborhoods, especially those long excluded from educational decision-making. At risk are the efforts themselves, which can be vulnerable to burnout, underfunding, or suppression by traditional power structures.

If expanded and supported, this model could redefine education as something communal, rooted, and transformative. If ignored, these hubs risk remaining isolated pockets of hope in an otherwise fractured landscape. This chapter explores what happens when the people rebuild the public good with their own hands.

"We stopped waiting for permission. We just started building."

Narrative Vignette

It started with a school garden. Then a free breakfast program. Then a mentorship collective run by local musicians and elders. Now, Ms. Diaz stands in what used to be the shuttered gym of Jefferson Middle School. It is alive again, converted into a learning and wellness hub.

Every weekday, children from across the neighborhood gather for integrated lessons taught by credentialed educators, community volunteers, and cultural workers. Mornings are for math, literacy, and science. Afternoons are for drumming, robotics, civic activism, and environmental stewardship. Parents stop by to use the food pantry or attend workshops on renters' rights. Elders tutor kids in the library. The building has become what it was always meant to be: a sanctuary for learning and care.

The state did not fund it. The community did.

Unpacking the Scenario

This future did not emerge from legislation. It was born from necessity, resistance, and love. As public institutions crumbled under political and economic pressure, families, educators, and organizers refused to let schools die quietly.

They took back buildings marked for demolition. They built cooperative learning hubs, anchored in cultural relevance, trauma-informed practices, and radical inclusion. They leveraged mutual aid networks, reallocated community funds, and forged partnerships with libraries, clinics, and universities. These were not just schools, they were commons: shared spaces stewarded for the public good.

In some regions, school boards tried to shut them down. In others, city councils recognized them as models of innovation. What they lacked in bureaucracy, they made up for in belonging.

Data Snapshot

- Between 2013 and 2023, hundreds of public schools in cities such as Chicago, Oakland, and Detroit were closed due to declining enrollment and budget deficits. In some cases, community-led efforts successfully repurposed these buildings into centers for adult learning, food distribution, and neighborhood support services (Kirshner et al., 2010; Pew Charitable Trusts, 2022).
- Community schools and learning hubs have been shown to improve student engagement and increase civic participation. A 2020 study by the Learning Policy Institute found that students in well-supported community school models experienced better attendance, academic performance, and social-emotional development (Maier et al., 2017).
- Food insecurity in neighborhoods served by school-based food distribution and mutual aid programs, such as Feeding America's School Pantry Program, decreased by an estimated 15% to 20%, according to internal program evaluations and national nonprofit reporting (Feeding America, 2023).
- Surveys conducted in districts with participatory school governance models, such as Oakland and New York City, indicate increased public trust and satisfaction with local education decision-making, especially among historically underserved families (Learning Policy Institute, 2021).

Voices from the Field

"We used to fight over what books to ban. Now we host banned book clubs and potlucks every Friday." - Khadijah M., student council leader, Philadelphia, PA

"I left teaching to work here. It is the first time in 15 years I have felt like an educator, not a test proctor." - Arturo J., educator, Salt Lake City, UT

"This is our school. Our people. Our rules. Our future." - Marisol D., grandmother and garden coordinator, Albuquerque, NM

Consequences

Civic Empowerment: Students grow up seeing democracy in action.

In the resilient commons, schools become more than academic institutions, they become living laboratories of democracy. Students participate in town halls, help draft classroom policies, and sit on advisory boards that shape real decisions. They grow up witnessing civic engagement not as a theoretical unit in social studies, but as a daily practice. Whether leading a budget forum or organizing a food drive, students learn that their voices carry weight. This is not just about leadership skills, it is about cultivating a generation that sees governance as something they do, not something done to them.

Redefined Success: Learning is measured through contribution, collaboration, and lived impact.

Traditional metrics, test scores, seat time, behavioral charts, take a back seat in these reimagined schools. Instead, success is measured by how students contribute to their communities, how they collaborate across difference, and how they apply learning to real-world challenges. A student might co-design a campus sustainability project or build a local history archive with elders. Their learning is validated not just by rubrics, but by impact. The question shifts from "Did you get an A?" to "Did your work matter?" And in that shift, both agency and purpose flourish.

Resistance to Austerity: These hubs shield communities from the worst effects of disinvestment.

In regions where state funding falters or public trust erodes, these civic-minded schools become anchors of stability. Community-run libraries, wellness clinics, food programs, and adult education courses find homes in reimagined school spaces. By leveraging public-private partnerships, mutual aid networks, and local volunteerism, these hubs resist the slow bleed of austerity. They do not replace public systems, but they refuse to surrender to their failure. And while the budget may be lean, the social capital is rich.

Scalability Challenges: Without systemic buy-in, these models remain hyper-local and unevenly distributed.

As promising as these models are, they often remain hyper-local, thriving in communities with the right mix of leadership, trust, and resources. Without systemic policy support or equitable funding streams, they struggle to scale. What works beautifully in one district may falter in the next due to state restrictions or staffing shortages. The danger is not failure, it is fragmentation. Without deliberate investment and coordination, these pockets of innovation risk becoming isolated islands of hope, rather than a movement that transforms public education at large.

Tension with Bureaucracy: Districts often view them as threats to traditional control structures.

District offices, accustomed to top-down control and rigid accountability models, often view these community-driven schools with suspicion. Questions about compliance, funding, and governance dominate the conversation. Innovators find themselves mired in red tape or sidelined by superintendents worried about precedent. In some places, these hubs are praised in public but undermined behind closed doors. The tension is real: one model demands flexibility and trust; the other demands uniformity and control. Bridging the two requires not just policy shifts, but a transformation in mindset.

What Could Be Done

- Pass legislation that funds and protects community-led public learning models.
- Create public infrastructure grants for school transformation projects.
- Encourage universities to form long-term, non-extractive partnerships with local schools.
- Shift education metrics to value wellbeing, civic engagement, and communal growth.

The Resilient Commons is not just a school. It is a declaration: that we will not abandon each other. That education belongs to all of us. And that the future is not inherited, it is built, together.

CHAPTER 5:

SURVEILLANCE SCHOOLS

"OBEDIENCE BY DESIGN"

Scenario Overview:

This scenario explores a future in which K-12 education is shaped by near-constant surveillance, where student behavior, attention, emotion, and communication are continuously monitored by AI-powered systems. The roots of this trajectory lie in zero-tolerance discipline policies from the 1990s and the post-Columbine expansion of school resource officers and metal detectors. In the 2010s and 2020s, the rise of edtech and concerns over school safety drove districts to adopt tools for digital monitoring, facial recognition, predictive analytics, and behavior scoring.

Today, this shift is propelled by surveillance tech companies, private security contractors, and data analytics firms. Federal and state grants have funded these systems under the banners of "school safety" and "student success." The logic: if we can monitor everything, we can prevent anything. But the lived result is something else entirely.

Beneficiaries include tech vendors, law enforcement consultants, and politicians seeking to appear "tough on discipline." At risk are students, particularly Black, Indigenous, LGBTQ+, disabled, and neurodivergent youth, who are disproportionately flagged by biased systems and subjected to dehumanizing interventions.

Left unchecked, this trajectory creates a schooling environment where compliance is valued over curiosity, where fear replaces trust, and where education becomes indistinguishable from social control. This chapter explores what happens when students are treated as potential threats, not people.

"I do not know if I am learning or just behaving the right way."

Narrative Vignette

Andre walks through the metal detector, places his school-issued tablet into the sensor tray, and scans his ID badge. The hallway lights shift from blue to green, today he has no demerits. Cameras track his gait, face, and posture. The system is watching for signs of agitation.

In class, he logs into his AI learning dashboard, which monitors typing speed, eye movement, and time on task. If his attention drifts, an automated nudge reminds him to focus. His digital behavior score is projected on a classroom leaderboard. He is ranked 17th out of 23.

After school, his mom gets an alert: "Andre showed signs of disengagement in math. Please review his dashboard." She shrugs. She is grateful there are no suspensions this month. At least, not yet.

Unpacking the Scenario

In this future, surveillance is framed as support. Edtech companies promise increased engagement, reduced behavioral issues, and optimized learning. Politicians sell it as accountability. Administrators say it prevents harm. But what it actually breeds is fear, self-censorship, and quiet compliance.

School surveillance began with cameras and metal detectors. Then came facial recognition, predictive policing tools, and AI-based monitoring of student emails and messages. During the 2020s, concerns about school violence and social unrest escalated the adoption of surveillance tech. Districts, under pressure, invested heavily.

By the early 2020s, behavior analytics had become embedded in nearly every layer of schooling, from hallways to home Wi-Fi. Discipline was increasingly managed through dashboards. Emotional nuance was reduced to data points. Privacy eroded, and trust eroded with it.

Data Snapshot

As of 2023, more than 80% of U.S. public high schools reported using security cameras to monitor student behavior, and nearly half used software to monitor online activity on school-issued devices (National Center for Education Statistics [NCES], 2023).

A 2024 study by the Center for Democracy & Technology found that students of color were more likely to be disciplined based on digital surveillance data, raising concerns about algorithmic bias and equity in school monitoring systems (Center for Democracy & Technology [CDT], 2024).

Major edtech companies have come under scrutiny for sharing student data, including behavioral profiles and browsing histories, with third-party vendors, often without clear parental consent or transparency about how the data is used (Cavanagh, 2023).

A 2023 report by the Brennan Center for Justice raised alarms about school districts piloting AI tools that monitor student communications and facial expressions under local safety initiatives, despite limited oversight or proven effectiveness (Brennan Center for Justice, 2023).

Voices from the Field

"We used to call it 'student support.' Now it feels like parole." - Jordan B., school counselor, Baltimore, MD

"My son was flagged for 'isolation risk' because he didn't speak in class. He's just shy." - Anita S., parent, Denver, CO

"These tools don't make school safer. They just make it quieter." - Malik T., senior student, Cleveland, OH

Consequences

Hyper-Policing of Youth: Minor behaviors become coded as threats, especially among marginalized students.

In surveillance-heavy schools, everyday behaviors, fidgeting, speaking out of turn, wearing a hoodie, are increasingly interpreted as risks. For marginalized students, especially Black and Brown youth, the line between disruption and danger is razor-thin. AI-driven threat assessment tools and anonymous reporting apps cast a wide net, but rarely interrogate the biases baked into their alerts. A student laughing too loudly in the hallway can trigger a lockdown drill. What once called for a conversation now calls for containment. And in the name of safety, childhood gets treated as a liability.

Erosion of Trust: Students internalize surveillance and self-censor out of fear of being flagged.

When students know they are being watched, they act like it. Surveillance does not just monitor, it modifies. Over time, students begin to self-censor, avoid asking hard questions, and suppress emotional expression. Vulnerability feels dangerous when every hallway has a camera and every search history is stored. Relationships with teachers shift, too; when educators are tasked with reporting behaviors to platforms instead of resolving them face-to-face, trust breaks down. Learning cannot flourish in a climate of suspicion, and neither can belonging.

Digital Profiling: Lifelong data trails shape student access to opportunities, often without transparency.

From keystroke logs to facial scans, today's student records go far beyond grades and attendance. Predictive software compiles behavioral patterns, academic performance, and engagement data into profiles that follow students across years, and sometimes across schools. Yet most families have no idea how this data is collected, interpreted, or used. A flagged pattern in 6th grade could influence access to an honors course in 10th. Without transparency or consent, students are judged not just for what they do, but for what algorithms predict they might do next.

Dehumanized Discipline: Interventions are automated, not relational or restorative.

Gone are the hallway conversations, the quiet check-ins, the restorative circles. In their place: auto-generated referrals, demerit tallies, and silent "behavior dashboards" reviewed in staff meetings. Systems that once relied on human context now act on coded behavior logs and predetermined thresholds. A student struggling with grief might be labeled "defiant." A child navigating a learning difference might be flagged as "noncompliant." Discipline is no longer something that happens with a student, it happens to them. And often, they don't even know why.

Equity Gaps Deepen: Predictive systems often reinforce racial and socio-economic biases.

Predictive discipline and behavioral analytics are not neutral. Studies show they often replicate and magnify existing biases, flagging students of color, English learners, and students with disabilities at disproportionate rates. When algorithms are trained on biased data, they do not just reflect inequality, they automate it. Meanwhile, students from affluent backgrounds are more likely to have their missteps interpreted as quirks or challenges, not threats. The same behaviors yield different consequences, and technology becomes a new layer of discrimination, with a digital veneer of objectivity.

What Could Be Done

- Enact student data privacy laws with strong enforcement mechanisms.
- Ban facial recognition and predictive behavior systems in K-12 settings.
- Invest in restorative justice programs and human-led conflict resolution.
- Shift school culture from control to care, where safety comes from community, not surveillance.

Surveillance does not equal safety. In the pursuit of order, we risk losing what makes schools places of growth: vulnerability, curiosity, and connection. The question is not what students are doing, but who we are asking them to become.

CHAPTER 6:

EDUCATOR EXODUS

"WHEN THE TEACHERS WALK AWAY"

Scenario Overview:

This scenario imagines a near future where mass teacher resignations have hollowed out the profession and destabilized the public education system. The seeds were planted decades ago, through chronic underfunding, rising class sizes, and the erosion of teacher autonomy. No Child Left Behind (2001) and Race to the Top (2009) imposed punitive accountability systems, while teacher pay stagnated relative to inflation. The COVID-19 pandemic accelerated burnout, with educators managing health risks, politicized curriculum battles, and a lack of institutional support.

The current drivers include austerity-minded legislatures, privatization advocates, and political actors who have weaponized culture war rhetoric to undermine trust in educators. Anti-union efforts and legislation restricting what teachers can say or do have further pushed professionals out of the field.

Those who benefit include charter networks hiring cheaper, less experienced labor; edtech companies offering automated instruction; and political groups eager to control public education narratives. At risk are students, especially those in marginalized districts, who face instability, unqualified instruction, and the loss of critical relationships.

If this trend continues, public education could become a skeleton of its former self: a space without continuity, mentorship, or morale. This chapter explores the human toll of systemic neglect and asks what happens when teachers are pushed past their breaking point.

"I did not leave the profession. The profession left me."

Narrative Vignette

Ms. Thompson's classroom still exists, on paper. Her name is listed on the school website, and automated emails go out under her address. But Ms. Thompson is gone.

She walked out mid-year, along with three other teachers at Carter Elementary. Her last straw? A student threw a chair, and there was no one to call. The school had no counselor, no admin coverage, and no behavioral support. She sat on the floor with the child for an hour until his grandmother arrived.

Now she works as an instructional designer for a tech company. She builds learning modules from a quiet home office and logs off by 5 p.m. Sometimes, she still dreams about her students. But she does not regret leaving. Her body stopped aching. Her mind is quiet.

At Carter, her students have had five substitutes in six weeks. None plan to stay.

Unpacking the Scenario

This is not a future dystopia, it is already underway. The educator workforce is in crisis. Low pay, high stress, politicized scrutiny, under-resourcing, and violence have turned teaching into a revolving door. As teachers leave in record numbers, schools fill gaps with non-certified staff, AI tools, or not at all.

During the 2020s, waves of state policies undermined teacher autonomy, banning books, mandating curriculum scripts, and criminalizing discussions on race, gender, and history. Meanwhile, salaries stagnated and healthcare benefits eroded. Teachers were asked to do more with less until many stopped doing it at all.

This scenario imagines what happens when the profession becomes unsustainable: schools hollow out, learning becomes transactional, and students lose trusted adult relationships that make education work.

Data Snapshot

- Between 2020 and 2024, an estimated 300,000 public school educators left the profession, with attrition rates disproportionately affecting schools serving low-income communities (National Center for Education Statistics [NCES], 2024; Education Week, 2023).
- By 2024-2025, North Carolina's overall teacher vacancy rate hovered around 7%, with rural and high-poverty districts reporting vacancy rates exceeding 20% in core subjects (North Carolina Department of Public Instruction [NCDPI], 2024; EdNC, 2024).
- Surveys conducted by the Learning Policy Institute and RAND Corporation found that the majority of teachers who left the profession cited burnout, poor working conditions, and lack of administrative support as primary reasons (Steiner et al., 2022; Learning Policy Institute, 2023).
- To address widespread vacancies, multiple states expanded the use of emergency teaching licenses and contracted virtual instructors from outside the state; a trend that raised concerns about instructional quality and educator preparedness (Barnum, 2023; RAND Corporation, 2023).

Voices from the Field

"It was not one thing, it was everything, all the time." - Jasmine R., former 5th grade teacher, Atlanta, GA

"I loved the kids. I hated what the system turned me into." - Devon M., former high school English teacher, Tulsa, OK

"The burnout is not just emotional. It is systemic. It is policy-driven." - Alicia T., education policy researcher, Washington, D.C.

Consequences

Mass Vacancies: Districts scramble to fill classrooms, often with underprepared substitutes or virtual monitors.

As educator burnout reaches crisis levels, districts across the country scramble to keep classrooms staffed. With certified teachers in short supply, many turn to long-term substitutes, virtual proctors, or even non-instructional personnel reclassified as "educators." In some schools, a single facilitator supervises multiple grade levels through online platforms. What students experience is not continuity of instruction but a revolving door of unfamiliar adults, patchwork lessons, and inconsistent expectations. The classroom becomes less a place of learning, and more a placeholder.

Lowered Standards: Hiring requirements are reduced, eroding quality and consistency.

To fill the gaps, states begin relaxing certification requirements, removing coursework mandates, loosening background checks, or issuing emergency licenses with minimal training. While framed as necessary flexibility, this shift erodes professional credibility and diminishes instructional quality. In some districts, new hires are given a laptop, a pacing guide, and little else. When preparation is treated as optional, and pedagogy as plug-and-play, students absorb the message: teaching is not a craft, it is a stopgap. And the long-term consequences are cumulative and corrosive.

Student Disruption: Constant turnover destabilizes learning environments and trust.

Every time a teacher leaves mid-year, or mid-week, students lose more than instruction. They lose routines, trust, and a sense of stability. Behavior spikes. Learning stalls. Classrooms feel less like communities and more like holding pens. For students who already face adversity outside of school, this instability can be especially damaging. And when turnover becomes the norm, students internalize the churn: adults do not stay, relationships do not last, and investment does not pay off. The emotional toll runs parallel to the academic one.

Loss of Mentorship: Students lose access to role models and advocates.

Great teachers are more than content experts, they are mentors, cultural translators, and lifelines. They notice the student who has not eaten. They pull aside the child who is retreating. They tell a young person, "I see something in you." When these educators walk away, they take far more than lesson plans. They take trust. And what replaces them, an app, a scripted lesson, a stranger, is not built to carry that emotional load. Students lose not just a teacher, but an advocate who might have changed their trajectory.

Downward Spiral: As conditions worsen, fewer enter the field, and more leave it.

Each resignation deepens the strain on those who remain. Class sizes swell. Planning periods vanish. Administrative pressure intensifies. The profession becomes less sustainable, less respected, and less appealing. Fewer young people pursue teaching. More veterans retire early. Aspiring educators are warned away by those already inside. What begins as a staffing challenge becomes a systemic unraveling. Without intervention, the cycle feeds itself, and public education becomes a workplace no one is willing to enter, and too many are desperate to leave.

What Could Be Done

- Establish competitive, regionally indexed teacher pay and benefits.
- Restore autonomy by removing punitive mandates and scripted instruction.
- Fund robust in-school mental health and behavioral support teams.
- Create teacher residencies and mentorship pipelines, especially for marginalized communities.

Teachers are not a renewable resource. When they walk away, it is not just a labor issue, it is a civic emergency. The future of public education depends on whether we are willing to rebuild not just classrooms, but the profession itself.

CHAPTER 7:

DEMOCRATIC RENAISSANCE

"RECLAIMING THE SCHOOLHOUSE AS A CIVIC POWERHOUSE"

Scenario Overview:

This scenario imagines a near future where communities refused to accept the hollowing out of public education and organized to reclaim schools as democratic spaces. The seeds were planted in decades of underfunding, stagnant pay, and policy overreach, but also in traditions of resistance where families, students, and educators fought to preserve public trust. The COVID-19 pandemic, while accelerating burnout, also revealed inequities that galvanized collective action.

The current drivers include grassroots coalitions, parent-student alliances, and educators who joined forces to resist privatization, censorship, and surveillance. They challenged austerity-minded legislatures, ran for school boards, and reframed governance as a shared civic responsibility.

Those who benefit include students who gain voice in shaping their education, educators who can align their expertise with democratic accountability, and communities that treat schools as hubs of civic life. At risk are the political actors and private interests who once profited from dismantling public trust.

If this trend continues, public education could be renewed as a cornerstone of democracy: a space where schools serve as engines of equity, sites of shared power, and places where civic trust is rebuilt from the ground up. This chapter explores what becomes possible when disillusionment gives way to collective action and the people closest to schools reclaim the right to define their future.

"They underestimated what happens when you give people a mic, a map, and a mission."

Narrative Vignette

Every folding chair in the middle school cafeteria is filled. Parents, students, elders, organizers, even the mayor, are gathered for the town's monthly education council meeting. At the front, fifteen-year-old Zara adjusts her slides. She is presenting her policy proposal to repurpose vacant school buildings as youth-led entrepreneurship incubators.

The crowd snaps, nods, and asks questions. Two retired educators offer to mentor the student planning team. A community member motions to fund the project with a local participatory budget. The council votes. It passes.

This is not a one-off. This is what school governance looks like now.

In the last five years, this district has elected a multiracial, multilingual school board, banned for-profit testing contracts, unionized substitute staff, and written a student bill of rights. It was not easy, but democracy rarely is.

REPURPOSING
SCHOOL
ROPERTIES
YOUTH COUNCIL
YOUTH RUN THIS
Student Power
Ban Test Contraces
Books Not Bots
BAN

Unpacking the Scenario

After decades of disillusionment, communities in this future reclaimed public education as the beating heart of democracy. In response to privatization, censorship, and surveillance, families, students, and educators organized, and won.

They ran for school board. They wrote policy. They took back state legislatures. And in doing so, they reframed education not as a service to be consumed, but as a public trust to be protected.

This democratic renaissance was not sparked by a single bill or billionaire. It was built through local organizing, student walkouts, mutual aid, and relentless community visioning. Trust was restored not through slogans, but through shared power.

Data Snapshot

- In recent years, grassroots coalitions advocating for public education, such as Support Our Schools and Red, Wine & Blue, have mobilized to contest school board races across multiple states, including Texas, Virginia, and Florida, with hundreds of candidates endorsed in 2022-2023 (Barnum, 2022; Klein, 2023).
- A 2023 report by the Brookings Institution found that family and community engagement in school decision-making, such as participatory budgeting and site-based councils, was correlated with increased civic trust and student engagement in historically underserved districts (Gross & Powell, 2023).
- Although students under 18 cannot legally vote in most school board elections, youth-led advisory councils and student board representatives have expanded in states like California, New York, and Illinois, providing students with formal roles in governance and policy feedback (NASBE, 2023).
- Illinois' "Whole Child Task Force" (est. 2021), New Mexico's Community Schools Initiative, and Minnesota's Full-Service Community Schools Grant are examples of legislation that grant families, educators, and community leaders structured input on public school funding, partnerships, and policies (Learning Policy Institute, 2023; NM PED, 2022; Minnesota DOE, 2023).

Voices from the Field

"When students realized they could write policy, not just be punished by it, everything changed." - Tanya R., youth organizer, Sacramento, CA

"I never thought I would run for office. Now I am writing the curriculum my grandkids will use." - Harold D., former custodian, Chicago, IL

"We fought for the right to be heard, and built something we never thought we could." - Zara M., student representative, Peñasco, NM

Consequences

Power Redistribution: Education decisions reflect those most impacted, students, teachers, families.

In the democratic renaissance, education governance no longer flows solely from state houses and central offices, it emerges from the people most affected by the system. Students sit on school boards with real voting power. Families co-create policy frameworks. Teachers help shape budgets and curricula. Decision-making becomes less about hierarchy and more about shared stakes. This redistribution does not happen easily, but when it does, schools become spaces of dignity and co-ownership, not top-down compliance. Power is no longer granted, it is reclaimed.

Policy Innovation: Bold, community-centered ideas replace corporate reform templates.

Rather than recycling corporate reform models or chasing tech trends, communities begin crafting bold, place-based policies rooted in justice, care, and collaboration. Districts launch restorative justice centers instead of expanding SRO programs. Public funds are directed toward housing supports, community schools, and multilingual programming. Pilot programs prioritize whole-child outcomes over test-based rankings. These are not tweaks, they are structural shifts. Innovation, in this future, is not about disruption for its own sake, it is about healing, imagination, and meeting human needs.

Civic Literacy Reborn: Students experience democracy not just as content, but as practice.

In this revitalized public system, democracy isn't confined to textbooks or simulations, it's lived. Students lead forums, negotiate class norms, draft school constitutions, and organize issue campaigns. They learn that democracy is messy, participatory, and powerful. Through practice, not performance, they gain the skills of public life: listening, dissenting, compromising, building. These aren't soft skills, they're survival skills for a pluralistic society. And when students graduate, they do so not just as test-takers, but as community shapers.

Public Trust Rebuilt: Transparency and participation reverse decades of institutional skepticism.

After decades of top-down reforms, data scandals, and disinvestment, communities begin to believe in public education again, not because they were convinced by a marketing campaign, but because they were invited back into the process. Transparency becomes the norm: budgets are public, decisions are co-authored, and mistakes are named, not hidden. Participation is not performative, it's expected. Over time, this openness turns suspicion into solidarity. Public schools are no longer seen as failing systems, they are understood as evolving commons worth investing in.

Increased Equity: Policies begin to reflect the needs of historically marginalized communities.

In this vision, equity is not a buzzword, it is a design principle. Policies are built from the margins, not just the center. Universal pre-K, trauma-informed teaching, language access, and inclusive curricula are not extras, they are baselines. Resource allocation reflects need, not privilege. Accountability shifts from punishing deficits to supporting growth. And as communities most harmed by past neglect step into power, schools begin to close opportunity gaps not with slogans, but with sustained, systemic change.

What Could Be Done

- Expand participatory budgeting in school districts.
- Ensure student, parent, and educator representation in all decision-making bodies.
- Pass legislation guaranteeing democratic school board governance and transparency.
- Embed civic engagement in every grade level, not as test prep, but as lived experience.

The schoolhouse is not just where democracy is taught, it is where it must be lived. If the past decades hollowed it out, this future shows how we can rebuild it from the ground up, louder, wiser, and more just than ever before.

CHAPTER 8:

THE FIGHT WE CHOOSE

"THE FORK IN THE ROAD IS OURS TO NAME"

Scenario Overview:

This chapter is different, it does not present a single scenario, but rather a convergence. It shows how all previous trajectories collide in the present: privatization accelerating, automation expanding, grassroots resistance building, and democratic renewal flickering. It is not a hypothetical future, it is a reflection of right now, framed as a critical decision point.

The idea that education stands at a crossroads is not new. But today's stakes are uniquely high. Federal and state policy choices, coupled with cultural division and economic instability, have created a moment where multiple futures are actively competing for dominance. Each pathway, surveillance, solidarity, abandonment, or rebuilding, is being written in real time by legislation, elections, organizing, and everyday choices in classrooms and communities.

Those who benefit from inaction include privatization advocates, anti-democratic forces, and extractive tech interests. Those who suffer are students, families, educators, and the broader public who rely on education as a pillar of civic life. But the fight is not over, and it is not passive.

This chapter challenges the you to move from reflection to agency. Futures are not inherited. They are constructed. The fight we choose will determine whether we preserve public education or reinvent it, or let it slip away entirely.

"We did not inherit this system. We shaped it. We can reshape it again."

Narrative Vignette

The screen splits in two. On one side: headlines about mass teacher resignations, budget shortfalls, and voucher expansions. On the other: footage of a youth-led march to the state capitol, signs held high: "Books not billionaires." "We are the curriculum." "Fully fund our futures."

Jamal scrolls past both. He is a high school junior in a district on the edge, caught between collapse and collective courage. His civics teacher assigns a project: envision your future school. Jamal sketches a place with gardens, elders, music, mental health rooms, and student-led electives. No walls, just open air and open minds.

He shares it at the school board's listening session. A parent from the other side of town applauds. A teacher nods. The superintendent invites him to join the youth advisory council. Jamal realizes: this is not a fight he has to watch. It is one he can join.

Unpacking the Scenario

This chapter is not one possible future. It is all of them, colliding in real time. The headlines of collapse coexist with grassroots movements. Hope and harm live side by side. The future is not chosen once, it is chosen daily.

This is where we are now. In a liminal moment where public education stands at a crossroads: further privatized, automated, and surveilled, or reclaimed, reimagined, and rebuilt through shared struggle.

The systems we live under are not inevitable. They were built by people, and they can be unbuilt and rebuilt, too.

Data Snapshot

- Public support for increased education funding has been notably strong in recent years. For instance, in Enfield, Connecticut, residents overwhelmingly backed a proposed $162 million budget for the 2025 fiscal year, which included a significant 5.57% increase in education funding. This support was driven by the community's desire to restore staff positions and programs cut in previous years (Enfield residents overwhelmingly supportive of increased education funding, 2025).
- Student activism has surged across the United States in recent years. Notably, in April 2025, hundreds of military-connected students at Department of Defense Education Activity (DoDEA) schools worldwide participated in walkouts protesting book bans and curriculum changes perceived as undermining diversity and inclusion efforts (Kheel & Novelly, 2025). Similarly, in February 2025, approximately 3,000 students from over 150 schools in the Houston Independent School District engaged in a mass sickout to protest state-appointed leadership and the implementation of AI-driven curricula (Houston ISD sees higher-than-average student absences during mass sickout protesting state takeover, 2025).

- Community organizations and mutual aid networks have increasingly stepped in to address educational disparities, often outperforming formal systems in promoting equity and innovation. For example, the Community Schools model integrates academics with health and social services, youth and community development, and community engagement, leading to improved student learning, stronger families, and healthier communities (Coalition for Community Schools, n.d.). Additionally, mutual aid networks have provided essential support during crises, such as the COVID-19 pandemic, by distributing resources and information to underserved communities (Curbed, 2020).
- A 2024 analysis by the Center for Information & Research on Civic Learning and Engagement (CIRCLE) found that youth voter turnout increased in 2022 midterm elections, with 27% of 18-29 year-olds participating; one of the highest rates in recent decades. This trend reflects growing youth interest in education-related policy and local decision-making (CIRCLE, 2024).

Voices from the Field

"We are not just fighting for schools, we are fighting for the soul of our democracy." - Renee C., education justice organizer, Chicago, IL

"Every act of resistance, no matter how small, is a blueprint for something better." - Samuel K., teacher, Oakland, CA

"I thought someone else would fix it. Then I realized: that someone is us." - Jamal T., student leader, Winston-Salem, NC

Consequences

Tipping Point Culture: Small choices, by students, voters, teachers, neighbors, accumulate into momentum.

The fight for public education doesn't hinge on a single sweeping reform, it builds through a thousand small acts. A student organizing a forum. A parent speaking at a board meeting. A teacher refusing to silence inclusive curriculum. A neighbor voting in a low-turnout election. Each action may seem minor in isolation, but together, they begin to bend the arc. Momentum doesn't arrive all at once, it gathers quietly, then breaks open. And when enough people choose to act, what once seemed impossible becomes inevitable.

Narrative Shift: The dominant story becomes not what we've lost, but what we're building.

For years, the dominant story has been one of loss, lost funding, lost trust, lost ground. But in this moment, the narrative turns. Communities begin to center what they are building: schools as healing spaces, classrooms as civic commons, students as co-authors of democracy. Media stories focus less on failure and more on resistance, renewal, and redesign. Language evolves. So does imagination. And when people start to believe that public education is not broken beyond repair, but broken open with possibility, they act accordingly.

Cross-Movement Solidarity: Education justice intersects with climate, labor, racial, and economic justice movements.

Education no longer exists in a silo. Organizers link arms with labor unions fighting for dignity, with climate activists pushing for sustainable schools, with racial justice advocates challenging systemic exclusion. Public education becomes a meeting ground, where movements overlap, where strategies align, where youth lead. The same systems that underfund schools often underpay workers, deny healthcare, and criminalize poverty. Solidarity becomes strategy. Together, these coalitions begin to build not just better schools, but a more just society.

Systemic Rebalancing: Public education becomes both the battlefield and blueprint for broader social transformation.

In this final scenario, public education is no longer treated as a downstream issue, it becomes the blueprint for systemic transformation. Universal childcare informs economic justice. Multilingual classrooms model cultural inclusion. Restorative practices challenge punitive systems far beyond school walls. What we do in schools echoes outward: shaping labor markets, public health, civic life. Education does not just reflect our values, it recalibrates them. And by rebuilding it with care and courage, we rebalance the system it holds up.

What Can Be Done

- Tell new stories: Amplify visions of justice-driven, community-rooted education.
- Organize locally: School board elections, teacher unions, student councils, parent coalitions.
- Vote for policies, not slogans, that restore, not replace, public systems.
- Teach resistance: Not just survival skills, but tools for systemic redesign.

The future is not fixed. It is fragile. It bends where we push. The question is no longer whether public education can be saved. It is whether we will choose to fight for the version worth saving.

A Blueprint in Fragments

In one future, Amira swipes into a learning hub sponsored by an oil company. In another, Elijah tests water quality in a forest microschool. Kyla talks to a screen instead of a teacher. Ms. Thompson walks away from a system that asked too much and gave too little. But Zara, the student council leader, stands before her school board with a proposal. And Jamal? He sketches a school that does not yet exist. He dares to believe it could.

These are not imagined futures. They are fragments of reality, pulled forward, stretched by the arc of current policy and political will. What lies ahead for public education is not fixed. It is fluid, malleable to the pressures we apply, the stories we tell, and the fights we choose.

Some will say the system is broken beyond repair. Others will insist it is working as designed. This book says: **the system is not finished.**

Every teacher who stays or leaves, every family that chooses public or private, every voter who shows up, or does not, nudges the system in one direction or another. School board elections, curriculum decisions, funding formulas, walkouts, community schools, voucher laws, book bans, student protests; these are not separate events. They are competing blueprints. They are live referenda on the soul of our democracy.

The truth is, we have never had a fully just or equitable public education system in this country. But we have always had the tools to build one. They are in our hands now more than ever.

What You Can Do Next?

You do not need a title or degree to shape the future of education. Start where you are:

- **If you are a student:** Join or form a student council. Attend a school board meeting. Interview your teachers. Write your own policy.
- **If you are a parent or caregiver:** Ask your school who decides how money is spent. Advocate for inclusive curriculum. Build coalitions with other families.
- **If you are an educator:** Stay if you can. If you cannot, stay connected. Mentor. Organize. Testify. Share your story.
- **If you are a neighbor or voter:** Vote in local school board and municipal elections. Reject apathy. Fund schools, not fear.

No one person can fix this. But every person can bend the path.

We do not need another round of top-down reforms. We need bottom-up, community-rooted, justice-driven transformation. We need courage. We need clarity. And we need each other.

The future is already here, in pieces. Let us gather them with purpose. Let us build something worth inheriting.

Blueprints for Action

Introduction

"What will you do with what you now know?"

This section is your bridge from reflection to action.

The scenarios in this book exposed multiple possible futures. Now, the **Blueprints for Action** offer hands-on guidance to help you respond, wherever you are.

These are not checklists. They are invitations.

Whether you are a student resisting censorship, a parent speaking out at a board meeting, an educator holding the line, or a policymaker committed to equity, you are part of something bigger. These blueprints are built for flexibility, urgency, and realism. You do not have to do everything. But you do have to start.

Each blueprint includes:

- A focused call to purpose
- Step-by-step guidance
- Questions and sentence starters
- Immediate, low-barrier actions to take today

This is not a solo fight. Bring people with you. Share these blueprints. Print them. Use them in meetings. Read them out loud. Translate them. Build on them. Leave no one out.

These are not perfect or complete. But neither is the world we are trying to build.

Let this be where your action begins.

Blueprint A: Students - Leading from the Inside

Part of the "Blueprints for Action" series

Why This Blueprint Exists

Public education does not just happen to you. It happens with and through you. Students have always been at the center of change, from walkouts to curriculum fights to organizing for justice. You are not the future. You are the present. And your leadership matters now.

This blueprint gives you the tools to lead, organize, and push for real change in your school. Not someday. Today.

Build a Student Council That Matters

What is the Problem? Many student councils are just for show. They plan spirit days but do not have real influence.

What You Can Do:

- Survey students, what issues matter most?
- Build a diverse organizing team (invite new voices).
- Write a mission statement focused on student voice and equity.
- Ask school leaders for official recognition and meeting time.
- Push for:
    - A voting seat on key school committees
    - A real student budget
    - Public forums for student ideas and feedback

Start Here Today:

"We believe our voices matter. We are requesting a recognized student council with input on decisions that affect us."

Organize a Campaign or Protest

What is the Problem? Maybe your school is banning books. Or enforcing unfair rules. Or ignoring student concerns.

How to Respond:

- Identify the problem clearly. Be specific.
- Gather a team. Assign roles: organizer, spokesperson, media, logistics.
- Plan your action: walkout, petition, posters, social media campaign.
- Collect evidence: quotes, stories, data.
- Practice safety and know your rights. Loop in trusted adults.

Sample Win: Students in Chicago successfully pushed their district to provide free menstrual products.

Sentence Starter:

"We are organizing because ____. We ask school leaders to ____ so that ____."

Write a Student Bill of Rights

Why It Matters: A strong school starts with shared values and protections, not just rules.

Steps to Take:

- Ask students: "What should every student have or be protected from?"
- Draft 5-10 rights. Use real stories and examples.
- Bring the list to your principal or school board.

Sample Rights:

- To be treated with dignity regardless of race, gender, or background
- To access mental health support
- To learn inclusive and accurate history
- To participate in decisions about school rules

Action Starter: Create a poster, zine, or short video with your Bill of Rights. Make it visible.

Learn the System. Change the System.

Power Tip: Real change means learning how the system works so you can push from the inside.

Key Actions:

- Attend a school board meeting. Speak during public comment.
- Learn how your school's money is spent. Ask questions.
- Write a student resolution or proposal.
- Educate others: create a "Know Your Rights" flyer or host a teach-in.

Questions to Ask:

- Who chooses our curriculum?
- What happens to unused budget money?
- How can students give formal input?

Start Today

Pick one step:

- Text 2 friends and ask what they would change about school
- Write your top 3 student rights
- Attend the next student council meeting, or start one
- Draft a flyer about an issue that matters to you

Final Reminder

You are not too young, too late, or too small to lead. Real change starts with you. **Power is not given. It is built.**

And you have already started.

Blueprint B: Parents & Families - Organize, Advocate, Protect

Part of the "Blueprints for Action" series

Why This Blueprint Exists

You do not have to be an expert to fight for your child. And you do not have to do it alone.

Parents and caregivers are often left out of school decisions, but you are essential to the system's success. This guide gives you the tools to organize with others, advocate for what matters, and protect public schools from the forces trying to dismantle them.

You are not just a parent. You are a stakeholder, a builder, and a protector.

Start a Parent Advocacy Group

Why It Matters: One voice can be ignored. Many voices create change.

Steps to Begin:

- Host a small meeting (home, library, community center).
- Identify 1-2 urgent issues: overcrowded classes, safety, censorship, underfunding.
- Start a communication group (WhatsApp, GroupMe, email).
- Invite diverse families, different languages, backgrounds, incomes.
- Create a short purpose statement.

Start Here Today:

"We are starting a group to speak up for our school community. Would you join us for a short meeting to talk about what matters to your family?"

Speak at School Board Meetings

Why It Matters: If you do not speak up, someone else will speak for you.

How to Prepare:

- Find the agenda online or request it ahead of time.
- Write a short statement (1-2 minutes max).
- Combine a personal story with one clear ask.
- Bring others, clap, document, show strength.

Template:

"My name is ___. I am a parent at ___. I am here tonight because ___. Our children deserve ___. I am asking the board to ___."

Repeat and Rotate: Make a schedule so different families speak at each meeting.

Monitor the Threats

Stay Informed:

- Follow your state's education bills (use sites like LegiScan).
- Watch for signs of:
    - Vouchers or ESAs
    - Book bans
    - Mass surveillance or behavior prediction software
    - Cuts to mental health, multilingual, or special education services

What You Can Do:

- Join your state PTA's advocacy group.
- Follow local education journalists and watchdog orgs.
- Meet your school board rep and state legislator.
- Bring stories, not just statistics.

Ask the Hard Questions

Any new program, app, or vendor, ask:

- Who profits from this?
- Was the community consulted?
- Is this accessible to all families?
- How will it affect student dignity and privacy?
- What alternatives were considered?

Write down responses and follow up. Transparency builds accountability.

Build Coalitions Beyond Your Circle

Do not just organize with people who think or look like you.

Try This:

- Host a multilingual potluck with childcare provided.
- Collaborate with student and teacher groups.
- Amplify the voices of families most impacted by injustice.
- Focus on shared values: respect, opportunity, community.

First Step: Invite someone you do not know well to help co-host your next meeting.

Start Today

- Pick one small step:
- Send a message to 3 parents you trust.
- Choose an issue that needs attention.
- Find the date of your next school board meeting.
- Ask one hard question about a school policy or program.

Final Reminder

Public education is not customer service, it is a public good. You are not a passive consumer. You are a defender of your community's future. And you do not have to act alone. Build the circle. Speak the truth. Protect what matters.

Blueprint C: Educators - Stay, Leave, or Transform

Part of the "Blueprints for Action" series

Why This Blueprint Exists

You are not just an employee. You are a steward of democracy, a cultivator of hope, and often the only adult some students trust. But the weight is real, and the system is pushing many out.

Whether you are staying, leaving, or somewhere in between, this guide is built for you: to protect your energy, sharpen your power, and remind you that you are not alone.

Teaching is not martyrdom. It is leadership. Let us treat it like it.

If You Stay: Protect Your Power

Know Your Rights & Resources:

- Read your contract closely. Know your grievance procedures.
- Document admin pressure, policy violations, and censorship attempts.
- Connect with your union, or organize one if you can.
- Build or join a local educator caucus (formal or informal).

Safeguard Your Joy:

- Claim one sacred period each week for creative or restorative teaching.
- Set digital and time boundaries, especially outside work hours.
- Cultivate relationships with students and families as sources of resilience.

Start Here Today:

"I am scheduling one block per week for joy-based teaching. No meetings. No tests. Just connection."

If You Leave: Do not Leave the Movement

You Are Not a Quitter. You Are a Witness.

Stay Connected by:

- Writing or speaking publicly about why you left
- Joining community schools, after-school programs, or mentoring orgs
- Supporting active educators through coaching or curriculum design
- Advocating for systemic change at the policy level

Aligned Job Paths:

- Instructional design
- Education journalism
- Youth development nonprofits
- Public service, educational advocacy, or community organizing

Starter Action: Host a storytelling night for former educators. Make the invisible visible.

Fight Censorship & Teach Truth

Facing Book Bans or Curriculum Gags?

- Know your state law's actual wording. Don't pre-censor.
- Embed truth into standards-based lessons using questions, not answers.
- Rely on primary sources, student inquiry, and analysis.
- Teach them how to think, not what to think.

Protect Yourself While Teaching Courageously:

- Plan collaboratively with trusted colleagues.
- Keep communication with families open and clear.
- Save your lesson plans and objectives as documentation.

Sentence Starter:

"This unit explores multiple perspectives on ___. Our goal is to practice analysis, empathy, and evidence-based thinking."

Practice Restorative Teaching

Shift from Punishment to Accountability:

- Replace detentions and referrals with circles, agreements, and dialogue.
- Involve students in shaping community norms and repair processes.
- Focus on healing, not control.

Starter Resources:

- *The Circle Way* - Kay Pranis
- *Restorative Practices Handbook* - Costello, Wachtel, & Wachtel
- *Teaching When the World Is on Fire* - Paul Gorski

Start Today

Pick one small shift:

- Join or message a fellow teacher about co-planning something subversive
- Replace one punitive rule with a community agreement
- Document one pressure point you have experienced this week
- Say no to unpaid work that does not serve students or justice

Final Reminder

You are not alone. You are not the problem. You are not powerless. You can stay. You can leave. You can transform. But wherever you are, you are part of something bigger.

Stay in the fight.

Blueprint D: School Board Members & Local Leaders - Govern with the People

Part of the "Blueprints for Action" series

Why This Blueprint Exists

You hold the levers of power. Not just over budgets and policies, but over trust, transparency, and the public's belief in education as a common good.

This guide offers tools for local officials, school board members, superintendents, city or county leaders, who want to govern with communities, not over them. You don't need a new program. You need a new approach.

The future of public education is being decided at your table. Make it count.

Launch Participatory Budgeting

Why It Matters: Most families, students, and even staff never see how decisions about money are made. Participatory budgeting (PB) gives them a real say.

How to Start Small:

1. Set aside a small portion of flexible funds ($10K-$50K).
2. Create a design team with students, staff, and families.
3. Host idea collection forums in multiple languages.
4. Facilitate a public vote.
5. Fund and implement winning ideas transparently.

Starter Phrase:

"This year, our district will co-create part of our budget with the community, because the people closest to the challenge often know the best solutions."

Guarantee Real Representation

Move Beyond Tokenism: Representation is not just showing up, it is shaping outcomes.

Best Practices:

- Give student reps real decision-making power
- Compensate students and caregivers for time and labor
- Rotate advisory councils with open, transparent recruitment
- Schedule meetings at accessible times with interpretation, childcare, and remote access

Quick Win: Host one meeting off campus at a library or community center to build trust.

Build an Equity-Centered Policy Framework

Use Equity as a Filter, Not a Buzzword.

Include Provisions That:

- Require equity impact statements for every major proposal
- Prohibit contracts with companies promoting surveillance or bias
- Mandate inclusive, culturally responsive curricula
- Explicitly protect LGBTQ+ students, students of color, disabled students, and multilingual learners

Resources:

- National Equity Project
- Dignity in Schools
- ACLU's Equity Lens Tools

Make Meetings Open and Meaningful

Design for Accessibility and Participation:

- Use plain language in agendas and communications
- Publish meeting materials ahead of time
- Rotate locations and livestream with captions
- Always include public comment, never bury it

Build Accountability:

- Publicly track district goals and report progress
- Respond publicly to patterns in community input
- Normalize dissent, democracy is not silence

Avoid the Technocratic Trap

Remember: You are not a CEO. This is not a boardroom. Schools are public goods, not private ventures.

Resist:

- Data dashboards that mask real harm
- Over-reliance on outside consultants
- "Efficiency" policies that cut care, connection, or creativity

Instead:

- Listen to lived experience
- Elevate qualitative and community evidence
- Share power, and trust people to use it well

Start Today

Choose one shift:

- Add a student/family voice to your next committee agenda
- Schedule a budget listening session
- Review your board's last five votes through an equity lens
- Replace jargon with plain language in your next newsletter

Final Reminder

You do not need all the answers, you need better questions, deeper partnerships, and the courage to co-govern with the people you serve.

This is not just school policy. It is democracy in practice.

Govern like it.

Blueprint E: Policy & Narrative Change - Shape the Big Picture

Part of the "Blueprints for Action" series

Why This Blueprint Exists

Every law is a story about values. Every budget is a statement of belief. Every headline shapes what people think is possible.

This blueprint is for advocates, organizers, creatives, and community members ready to shift public education from a story of scarcity and crisis to one of dignity, justice, and collective power.

You don't need a title to shape policy. You just need strategy and voice.

Frame the Fight

Shift the Narrative:

- From "schools are failing" → to "schools are being failed by disinvestment, division, and disinformation."
- From "school choice" → to "public dollars belong in public schools."
- From "efficiency" → to "education that centers care and humanity."

Affirm What Matters:

- Education is a public good, not a product.
- Local communities deserve power, not corporate intermediaries.
- Every child deserves safety, joy, and opportunity.

Start Here Today:

Use these reframes in your conversations, social posts, or letters to the editor.

Reclaim the Language

Glossary Shift for Equity-Minded Advocacy:

- Accountability → Community transparency
- Rigor → Relevance + Relationships
- Innovation → Grassroots imagination
- Choice → Equity, not exclusion

Tip: When you hear coded language (like "parental rights"), ask: Whose rights? At whose expense?

Ask Smarter Questions

For Elected Officials or Candidates:

- Will you oppose private school vouchers and protect public funding?
- Do you support inclusive curriculum and educator autonomy?
- How will you center student, family, and teacher voices in decision-making?
- What is your plan for mental health and holistic support, not just test scores?

For the Media:

- Who benefits from this policy, and who is at risk?
- Are student voices included?
- Is this story reinforcing stereotypes or highlighting solutions?

Use Your Platform (Big or Small)

Write or Speak Publicly:

- Submit op-eds or letters to the editor after school board decisions
- Tell your story as a student, teacher, or family member
- Collaborate on joint statements or campaigns with others

Start a Campaign:

- Use hashtags like #FundOurFutures, #WeAreTheCurriculum, #NoMoreBans
- Highlight wins and joy, not just harm
- Tag decision-makers and media outlets

Use Local Media Strategically:

- Pitch a story about a community-led school success
- Build relationships with education reporters

Connect Across Movements

Education intersects with everything: housing, labor, climate, disability rights, racial justice.

Ways to Build Together:

- Co-host events with climate, health, or housing groups
- Partner with labor unions to protect school staff and pay equity
- Link youth-led organizing to broader civic movements

Core Message: Public education is part of every liberation struggle. Treat it that way.

Start Today

Choose one action:

- Write a tweet reframing a harmful education narrative
- Ask your local candidate where they stand on vouchers
- Partner with another movement group for a joint teach-in
- Submit a letter to the editor about a local education issue

Final Reminder

You do not need access to a podium to speak powerfully. You do not need a seat in office to shape policy.

Start where you are. Speak the truth. Change the story.

And the future will follow.

Resource List - Tools for the Fight Ahead

"We do not have to start from scratch. We just have to start, together."

This curated list connects you to organizations, tools, and resources aligned with the vision of justice-centered public education outlined in this book. Whether you are a student, educator, parent, policymaker, or advocate, these links can help turn learning into action.

General Public Education Advocacy

- Network for Public Education - National coalition defending public schools against privatization.
    - networkforpubliceducation.org
- Journey for Justice Alliance - Grassroots groups building community-driven, sustainable school models.
    - j4jalliance.com

Youth-Led Organizing

- Student Voice - Platform for youth-led education advocacy, research, and organizing tools.
    - stuvoice.org
- IntegrateNYC - Student-designed framework for integrating and transforming schools.
    - integratenyc.org

Parent & Family Organizing

- ParentsTogether - Campaigns and toolkits for families advocating around education, equity, and economic justice.
    - parentstogether.org
- National Parents Union - Organizing hub for family-led movements pushing for equity and accountability.
    - nationalparentsunion.org

Educator Networks & Tools

- **Badass Teachers Association** - Educator advocacy network challenging corporate ed reform and fighting for justice.
    - badassteacher.org
- **Zinn Education Project** - Free, people's history resources and campaigns to teach truth.
    - zinnedproject.org
- **Rethinking Schools** - Publisher and professional network advancing social justice in education.
    - rethinkingschools.org

Policy, Narrative, & Research

- **Public Funds Public Schools** - Legal and policy watchdog tracking vouchers and ESA laws.
    - pfps.org/home
- **Dignity in Schools Campaign** - National coalition challenging the school-to-prison pipeline through model policy and advocacy.
    - dignityinschools.org
- **National Equity Project** - Tools and coaching for equity-centered school leadership.
    - nationalequityproject.org
- **The Education Trust** - Research and advocacy for closing opportunity gaps across race and income.
    - edtrust.org

Democracy & Civic Engagement

- Participatory Budgeting Project - Toolkits for implementing democratic school and district budgeting.
  - participatorybudgeting.org
- Ballot Ready - Local ballot breakdowns for school board and education-related races.
  - ballotready.org
- Vote.org - Nonpartisan voter registration and turnout tools for families and youth.
  - vote.org

These are not the only organizations doing this work, but they are some of the most trusted, actionable, and aligned with a vision of public education that is democratic, equitable, and rooted in community.

Use them. Join them. Build with them.

Call to Collective Action

This is the moment we decide what kind of future we are willing to build, and what we are no longer willing to accept.

If you made it this far, you know the stakes. You have seen how our public schools are being shaped by agendas that value profit over people, control over curiosity, division over democracy. But you have also seen the possibilities, the forks in the road where we could choose justice, equity, and belonging.

The question is not just what will happen. It is who will shape what happens next.

This book was never meant to be read in isolation. It is meant to be used. Shared. Debated. Rewritten in practice. Every scenario is already unfolding somewhere. Every blueprint can be picked up and adapted. Every blueprint is a starting point for organizing, not an end.

If you are a student, ask a harder question. Speak up even if your voice shakes. If you are a teacher, protect your joy and your truth. If you are a parent, show up, even when you are tired. If you are a board member, go beyond policy. Build trust. If you are in the movement, connect the dots. Share your light.

You do not have to do it all. But you do have to do something.

Start with one conversation. One poster. One petition. One story.

Then keep going.

Because we are not just defending public education. We are defining it.

And if we do it together, we just might win.

- Derek Setser

My Commitments to Public Education

This is not just a book. It is a beginning. Use this page to clarify what you are willing to stand for, and what you are ready to do.

What do you believe about public education? (Write 1-2 sentences that reflect your core values.)

What will you speak up about, even when it is hard? (A policy, a practice, or an injustice you are no longer willing to accept silently.)

What action will you take in the next 30 days? (Be specific: join a group, attend a meeting, write an article, host a conversation.)

Who will you bring with you? (Name one person you will invite into this work, student, colleague, neighbor, or friend.)

Signature: _____

Date: _____

Make a copy. Post it somewhere visible. Revisit it often. Update it when needed. This is yours to own, and to live.

Facilitation Guide for Book Clubs & Communities

This guide is designed to support group discussion, reflection, and collective action. Use it with educators, students, families, or community leaders, whether in living rooms, classrooms, or school board work sessions.

General Facilitation Tips

- Rotate who leads each discussion to build shared ownership.
- Pair personal stories with policy analysis.
- Use a community agreement (e.g., speak from the "I," listen with humility, protect vulnerable stories).
- Build in time for silence, journaling, or drawing.
- Don't skip the action step, reflection without movement serves no one.

Discussion Questions by Scenario Chapter

1. The Privatized Nation - "Voucher Victory"

- What parts of this scenario are already showing up in your community?
- How do vouchers or ESAs affect equity?
- Who benefits from privatization, and who's left out? Action Prompt: Research the most recent voucher legislation in your state. What's the public cost?

2. Microschool America - "Fragmentation"

- How does microschooling show up in your community?
- What freedoms does it offer? What inequalities might it deepen?
- What happens to the idea of a shared public education? Action Prompt: Compare microschool access across two different zip codes in your area.

3. AI Replaces Us - "Automation Overreach"

- Where has tech begun to replace teachers in your district?
- What are the trade-offs between convenience and connection?
- Who profits when AI replaces human educators? Action Prompt: Interview students or educators on how AI has changed classroom life.

4. The Resilient Commons - "Community Rebuilds"

- What local efforts give you hope for public schools?
- Who is already rebuilding education from the ground up?
- What would a commons approach to education look like in your district? Action Prompt: Visit or highlight one public school/community partnership doing things differently.

5. Surveillance Schools - "Control and Compliance"

- How is student or staff behavior currently monitored?
- What is the emotional cost of constant tracking?
- What is the difference between care and control? Action Prompt: Host a conversation about student privacy and digital rights.

6. Educator Exodus - "Burnout Crisis"

- Why are teachers leaving?
- What is being done in your district to retain staff?
- What would a sustainable profession look like? Action Prompt: Survey educators in your community about their biggest pain points, and publish the results.

7. Democratic Renaissance - "Hope Reclaimed"

- Where have grassroots wins already occurred?
- What does authentic community leadership look like?
- How can education be democratized, not just delivered? Action Prompt: Create a local coalition to track education board elections and policies.

8. The Fight We Choose - "A Call to Action"

- What spoke to you in this closing chapter?
- What feels most urgent, and what feels most possible?
- What's your personal entry point into the work? Action Prompt: Fill out your public pledge and invite three others to do the same.

Closing Discussion Prompts

- What chapter left the strongest impression? Why?
- What connections do you see between scenarios?
- How does this book change how you see your role in education?
- What will your next step be, and who will take it with you?

Use this guide to organize locally, reflect deeply, and act collectively. Our future is not something to inherit. It's something we build.

Glossary of Key Terms:

Public Education - A system of schooling funded and governed collectively to serve the public good, not private interests.

Voucher / ESA - A policy that redirects public funds to private or religious schools, often at the expense of public education systems.

Microschool - A small, often unregulated educational setting formed by families, educators, or entrepreneurs outside traditional school structures.

Hollow State - A term describing the outsourcing of public services to private entities, leading to loss of public accountability.

Surveillance Capitalism - The monetization of personal data through technology systems, often without informed consent.

Commons - Shared resources and governance built and protected by community, not controlled by markets or the state.

Restorative Practice - A non-punitive approach to addressing harm and building community by focusing on repair rather than punishment.

Participatory Budgeting - A democratic process in which community members directly decide how to allocate part of a public budget.

Narrative Shift - A strategic reframing of dominant cultural stories in order to build new social or political realities.

References:

AP News. (2023, October 2). North Carolina expands school voucher program to allow all families to apply. https://apnews.com/article/north-carolina-school-vouchers-2023

Barnum, M. (2022, November 10). What the school board election results say about the future of public education. Chalkbeat. https://www.chalkbeat.org/2022/11/10/school-board-election-results-2022

Barnum, M. (2023, October 11). Schools increasingly rely on virtual teachers to fill vacancies. Experts raise equity concerns. Chalkbeat. https://www.chalkbeat.org

Brennan Center for Justice. (2023). The dangers of facial recognition and AI surveillance in schools. https://www.brennancenter.org/our-work/research-reports/ai-surveillance-schools

Cavanagh, S. (2023, March 7). Ed-tech privacy concerns grow as student data is shared with third-party vendors. Education Week. https://www.edweek.org/technology/ed-tech-privacy-concerns-grow-as-student-data-is-shared-with-third-party-vendors/2023/03

Center for Democracy & Technology. (2024). The impact of student surveillance: Disproportionate discipline and digital profiling in U.S. schools. https://cdt.org/insights/the-impact-of-student-surveillance-in-schools/

Center for Information & Research on Civic Learning and Engagement (CIRCLE). (2024, March 28). Young voters made a difference in 2022 midterm elections: Analysis and trends. Tufts University. https://circle.tufts.edu/latest-research/youth-voting-2022-midterms

Coalition for Community Schools. (n.d.). What is a community school? https://www.communityschools.org/what-is-a-community-school/

Curbed. (2020, June 23). Mutual aid networks and coronavirus: Is it enough to just be neighbors? https://archive.curbed.com/2020/6/23/21294321/mutual-aid-societies-nyc-pandemic

Doan, B., Asanjarani, A., Tuma, A., Diliberti, M., & Kaufman, J. H. (2024). Artificial intelligence in K-12 education: Current uses and concerns (RR-A2162-2). RAND Corporation. https://www.rand.org/pubs/research_reports/RRA2162-2.html

EdNC. (2024, January 10). Teacher vacancies remain high as legislative funding shifts toward private education. https://www.ednc.org

Education Week. (2023, March 1). The big quit: Why teachers are leaving the profession in record numbers. https://www.edweek.org

Enfield residents overwhelmingly supportive of increased education funding. (2025, May 1). CT Insider. https://www.ctinsider.com/journalinquirer/article/ct-enfield-budget-education-schools-20302593.php

Feeding America. (2023). School Pantry Program: Reducing child hunger where children learn. https://www.feedingamerica.org

Florida Policy Institute. (2023, August 24). Vouchers expand to students already in private schools, shifting public dollars away from public schools. https://www.floridapolicy.org

Grand View Research. (2024). Artificial intelligence in education market size, share & trends analysis report by deployment, by technology, by application, by end-user, by region, and segment forecasts, 2024-2030. https://www.grandviewresearch.com/industry-analysis/artificial-intelligence-in-education-market

Gross, B., & Powell, D. (2023). Family and community engagement: A lever for school improvement. Brookings Institution. https://www.brookings.edu/research/family-and-community-engagement-a-lever-for-school-improvement

Hamilton, L. (2023, February 23). Why some Black families are choosing to homeschool. Time Magazine. https://time.com/6257407/black-homeschooling-parents/

Houston ISD sees higher-than-average student absences during mass sickout protesting state takeover. (2025, February 6). Houston Chronicle. https://www.houstonchronicle.com/news/houston-texas/education/hisd/article/hisd-student-sickout-absences-20232391.php

Kheel, R., & Novelly, T. (2025, April 10). Hundreds of students at military base schools walk out to protest diversity crackdown. Military.com. https://www.military.com/daily-news/2025/04/10/were-going-fight-what-we-believe-military-kids-protest-diversity-crackdown-base-schools-worldwide.html

Kirshner, B., Gaertner, M., & Pozzoboni, K. (2010). Tracing transitions: The effect of school closures on displaced students. Educational Evaluation and Policy Analysis, 32(3), 407-429. https://doi.org/10.3102/0162373710376823

Klein, A. (2023, February 8). Inside the movement to flip school boards in favor of public education. Education Week. https://www.edweek.org/leadership/inside-the-movement-to-flip-school-boards-in-favor-of-public-education/2023/02

Learning Policy Institute. (2017). Community schools as an effective school improvement strategy: A review of the evidence. https://learningpolicyinstitute.org/product/community-schools-effective-school-improvement-brief

Learning Policy Institute. (2021). The role of community schools in place-based education transformation. https://learningpolicyinstitute.org

Learning Policy Institute. (2023). The role of community schools in place-based education transformation. https://learningpolicyinstitute.org/product/community-schools-place-based-education

Learning Policy Institute. (2023). Understanding teacher shortages: Why teachers leave and how to support them to stay. https://learningpolicyinstitute.org

Maier, A., Daniel, J., Oakes, J., & Lam, L. (2017). Community schools as an effective school improvement strategy: A review of the evidence. Learning Policy Institute. https://learningpolicyinstitute.org/product/community-schools-effective-school-improvement-report

Minnesota Department of Education. (2023). Full-Service Community Schools Grant. https://education.mn.gov/MDE/dse/fulsrvcs

National Association of State Boards of Education (NASBE). (2023). Student representation in school governance. https://www.nasbe.org/student-voice-school-governance/

National Center for Education Statistics (NCES). (2023). Homeschooling in the United States: 2021-22. U.S. Department of Education. https://nces.ed.gov

National Center for Education Statistics. (2023). School safety and security measures: 2019-20 school year. U.S. Department of Education. https://nces.ed.gov/programs/coe/indicator/a19/school-safety-security

National Center for Education Statistics. (2024). Digest of Education Statistics, 2023. U.S. Department of Education. https://nces.ed.gov

National Home Education Research Institute. (2023). Homeschooling growth trends post-2020. https://www.nheri.org/research

New Mexico Public Education Department (NM PED). (2022). Community Schools Strategy. https://webnew.ped.state.nm.us/bureaus/community-schools

North Carolina Department of Public Instruction. (2024). 2023-24 Educator Vacancy Report. https://www.dpi.nc.gov

North Carolina Department of Public Instruction (NCDPI). (2024). Generative AI in North Carolina classrooms: Guidance and best practices. https://www.dpi.nc.gov/media/ai-classroom-guidance

Office of the Arizona Governor. (2024, March 15). Governor's budget briefing: ESA expenditures top $600 million. https://azgovernor.gov/news/esa-budget-2024

Pew Charitable Trusts. (2022). Repurposing closed school buildings: Opportunities for community revitalization. https://www.pewtrusts.org

RAND Corporation. (2023). Teachers' views on the state of public education: Findings from the American Teacher Panel. https://www.rand.org

Ray, B. D. (2023). African American homeschool parents' motivations: Safety, culture, and achievement. Journal of School Choice, 17(1), 45-61. https://doi.org/10.1080/15582159.2023.2173268

Southern Poverty Law Center & Education Law Center. (2023, July). The cost of choice: How voucher programs fail students with disabilities. Public Funds Public Schools. https://pfps.org

Steiner, E. D., Doan, S., & Woo, A. (2022). Teacher well-being and intent to leave: Insights from the 2022 State of the American Teacher Survey. RAND Corporation. https://www.rand.org/pubs/research_reports/RRA1108-6.html

VELA Education Fund. (2023). Annual Impact Report. https://velaedfund.org/impact

www.ingramcontent.com/pod-product-compliance
Lightning Source LLC
Chambersburg PA
CBHW070636030426
42337CB00020B/4043